With Love Somehow

TONY CONNOR

With Love Somehow

POEMS

LONDON
OXFORD UNIVERSITY PRESS
NEW YORK TORONTO
1962

Oxford University Press, Amen House, London E.C.4

GLASGOW NEW YORK TORONTO MELBOURNE WELLINGTON
BOMBAY CALCUTTA MADRAS KARACHI LAHORE DACCA
CAPE TOWN SALISBURY NAIROBI IBADAN ACCRA
KUALA LUMPUR HONG KONG

PRINTED IN GREAT BRITAIN
AT THE UNIVERSITY PRESS, OXFORD
BY VIVIAN RIDLER
PRINTER TO THE UNIVERSITY

CONTENTS

vii

ACKNOWLEDGEMENTS

These poems were written between 1957 and 1961. The most recent are 'For a Lost Girl', but the rest are not in chronological order.

Acknowledgements are due to the editors of *Ambit*, *Outposts*, and *Poetry and Audience*, in which some of them first appeared, and to the editor of *The Noble Savage* who printed my 'Twelve Love Poems' in the fourth number of that magazine. This sequence appears here as 'For a Lost Girl', with poems three and nine omitted at the request of the present publisher.

END OF THE WORLD

THE world's end came as a small dot
    at the end of a sentence. Everyone died
without ado, and nobody cried
    enough to show the measure of it.

God said: 'I do not love you', quite
    quietly, but with a final note;
it seemed the words caught in his throat,
    or else he stifled a yawn as the trite

phrase escaped his dust-enlivening lips.
    At least, there was no argument,
no softening tact, no lover's cant,
    but sudden vacuum, total eclipse

of sense and meaning. The world had gone
    and everything on it, except the lives
all of us had to live: the wives,
    children, clocks which ticked on,

unpaid bills, enormous power-blocks
    chock-full of arms demanding peace,
and the prayerful in a state of grace
    pouncing on bread and wine like hawks.

THREE WINTER WALKS

ONE

TAKE the street where the cinders crunch,
where a leaning gaslamp's splinters
haunt a cat's eyes, green as bile,
cold as the winter's.
While the heavy shoulders hunch,
and the soot-stained snowflakes pile,
hear the voices in the air:
'These streets lead nowhere, nowhere.'

Summon the echoes from the brew:
no one, not a soul, will bother.
Flagstoned ages lie beyond
this frozen smother.
And the streets you thought you knew
shift, and break the easy bond,
hear the voices in the air:
'These streets lead nowhere, nowhere.'

Every house is bolted tight,
every street has slipped its tether,
all the world's gone to its bed
but you and the weather.
No wise men will come tonight,
not a star shine overhead.
Hear the voices in the air:
'These streets lead nowhere, nowhere.'

TWO

ONE that would make the frenzied echoes die
paced the dark cobbled streets,
but found no silent place.
A dog barked in his face,
and, flapping like mad sheets,
he saw the dead about the graveyard fly.

Whether they flew for him or for some other
he did not stop to think,
being preoccupied
with the earth's other side.
A shadowed woman winked,
but she was flesh and very like his mother.

Under a lamp he marked his steaming breath
and wondered at its weight.
Pouring from public bars
harsh laughter tore his scars,
but supper would not wait.
The street ran on to someone else's death.

THREE WINTER WALKS

THREE

I WALKED one night by the old Methodist Cemetery,
my brain turbulent with sound but my heart empty.
On one side the roller-skating rink and the Globe cinema
shabby from long disuse, murmured like unquiet dreamers;
across the street, beyond broken railings, gaslight tangled
slant crosses, cherubs, outstretched stained arms of angels.

Knowing that each man's God dies with that man,
I anticipated no commerce with spirits, feared no phantom,
was sure I trod in the lee of my own singularity,
between a book and bed, walking the sleeping city.
Until, on the main road, where the sodium lights effaced
the bulk of the present, I came upon a ghost.

It looked like my own reflection, bruised, darkly shadowed,
and spoke from the toyshop window, saying: 'You are cardboard.
A cardboard figure ingeniously contrived in the semblance
of all you have forfeited; I am the evidence—
the unadmitted metaphor of your failure,
guardian of divested talents, and your rightful creature.'

I opened my mouth to speak, but through my mind,
tumbling the ready answers, blew a rain-bearing wind
that tossed me about, and tore my lips to a hole
through which it left, spiralling papers up Cheetham Hill.
The ghost stood quietly by, then, fleshed completely,
said: 'Once you were rich in love; have you missed it lately?

'No, for it is with your heart; not empty, but thrown away,'
and I saw my heart inside him, struggling as though to be free.
'Look', he said, 'at the gifts you trampled in gutters;
I am mighty with splendours you could not trouble to nurture:
faith, compassion, the truth that needs a brave advocate—
all the squandered assets of your inherited estate.'

4

A wet gust plastered me to the glass, spreadeagled,
compelling my eyes to suffer the throbbing dazzle
from which he spoke again, in a thousand mingling voices:
'These are the poems you might have written; the choices
ignored in favour of quick returns and popularity,
or the thick-roofed, stout-walled, home-sweet-home of self pity;

'Listen: they cry for what they have been denied,
being both unaccommodated and disembodied.
This is worst of all, that you, their natural servant
and master too, have broken the holy covenant
between a man and what he is gifted to body forth;
it remains now for them to witness your lonely death.'

Gripped then by the taloned wind, I was torn to shreds,
to tumble and flap in corners, slop towards grids
bright bits of words staining a black gurgle,
while a segment of smile chased teeth up Cheetham Hill.
Spinning away in my mind, I heard the ghost
whisper to rows of toys: '. . . And this death is saddest.'

After (or was it in memory), I walked in Thomas Street,
by the side of the graves, the dead beyond dispute,
where a shadowed policeman flashing a torch like a glow-worm
assured himself that no locks were broken, no harm
befell the roller-skating rink and the Globe cinema:
those murmurers by the graves, those unquiet dreamers.

A RATHER PUBLIC STATEMENT

I DO not intend to contribute
a single line, any half-heard
snatch of mystery
to the street's chronicle.
I am deaf among men;
I am dumb among women;
I am the prince of never-there,
the master of winter.

I have no knowledge to offer
about the marriage bed,
nor am I able to say
where, or why important
decisions were made
affecting the lives
of all who heard them
and many more who did not.

I will not pretend an ability
to judge character from faces;
darkness frightens me
and I am apprehensive in sunlight.
Nevertheless,
mine was the bland smile,
the fur coat of incomprehension
in the catastrophe.

When the trek ended, frustrated
by the abattoir wall,
and the disgusted others
started rewinding the string,
I was in the chip shop
ordering fourpenn'orth.
I had not come all that way
for nothing.

On certain nights I have discerned
complicated patterns
in smudged penumbras,
but have never missed my supper.
The voices from alleys
—loving or hating—
I have accepted as part
of a wholesome definition.

You will appreciate my reluctance
to give you directions:
my inability to reach
the homes of others
is widely known—
although one of my hobbies
is studying maps
in the front room.

Finally, let me assure those
who imagine me lending a willing ear,
that my lopsided appearance
is congenital,
and should not be interpreted
as a leaning
towards anything
other than the ground.

AUTUMN

October's cache receives Summer.
Under creaking branches bared to rain
wet wads of leaves clog the gutter.
The chimney-breast darkens with a stain

no fire can dry. Evening mists smother
whatever I saw clearly last week:
the street's end, a faithful lover,
where I am going, words to speak

which mean the same in all weathers.
A general death enters the head
through aches that seem to augur fevers,
and muffled dreams in a heaped bed

there's no warming. Reduced to lumber,
the mind's big sun, ease of sense,
are scoured out, as though in a manner
they were the disastrous trappings of innocence,

known for deception, and thrown over.
What is bad bids to be worse,
and nothing to do but crouch and shudder
over the gaping, rifled purse.

you trusted with riches, in a corner
burrowed from slashing wet, harsh gust,
while all through the house smug phantoms mutter
of times too severe for them to outlast.

INVASION OF THE HOUSE

THIN in the ear as a bat's squeak,
   and through the house all night like bats swarming,
   dodging and darting from room to room—
a piped pattern upon the dark hours—
   is the laughter, the moan, the disturbed talk
of all the household gods. The flowers

loll on the landing. From her bed
   the mother of many men (seventy years—
   and thirty of them widowed—bleared
to whistling breath and no voice) raises
   a hand in the face of the crowding dead,
summoning sons that have never known her praise

to lean to her mouth from the world's end
   that, if there's strength enough, she may revile
   each and every one: the cruel
issue of love. Young stay-at-home awakes
   suddenly at the pushed sheets' small sound;
chair-cramp forgotten, his headache

in someone else's skull where shrill
   laughter and howls of grief and busy chatter
   swoop from the rafters' gloom, then scatter.
His mother lies, fists clenched, face set
   to a fierce stare, as if in death her will
survived, like the growth of grey beneath her hair-net.

Kingdoms away, in the next room,
   awkwardly swagged and heavy with chirruping dreams,
   his young wife sleeps, her moist palms
against her belly's hump, wherein there stirs
   the son eager to quit the womb,
and get at her breasts, and share this house of hers.

ELEGY FOR ALFRED HUBBARD

Hubbard is dead, the old plumber;
who will mend our burst pipes now,
the tap that has dripped all the summer,
testing the sink's overflow?

No other like him. Young men with knowledge
of new techniques, theories from books,
may better his work straight from college,
but who will challenge his squint-eyed looks

in kitchen, bathroom, under floorboards,
rules of thumb which were often wrong;
seek as erringly stopcocks in cupboards,
or make a job last half as long?

He was a man who knew the ginnels,
alleyways, streets—the whole district,
family secrets, minor annals,
time-honoured fictions fused to fact.

Seventy years of gossip muttered
under his cap, his tufty thatch,
so that his talk was slow and clotted,
hard to follow, and too much.

As though nothing fell, none vanished,
and time were the maze of Cheetham Hill,
in which the dead—with jobs unfinished—
waited to hear him ring the bell.

For much he never got round to doing,
but meant to, when weather bucked up,
or worsened, or when his pipe was drawing,
or when he'd finished this cup.

I thought time, he forgot so often,
had forgotten him, but here's Death's pomp
over his house, and by the coffin
the son who will inherit his blowlamp,

tools, workshop, cart, and cornet
(pride of Cheetham Prize Brass Band),
and there's his mourning widow, Janet,
stood at the gate he'd promised to mend.

Soon he will make his final journey;
shaved and silent, strangely trim,
with never a pause to talk to anybody: how arrow-like, for him!

In St. Mark's Church, whose dismal tower
he pointed and painted when a lad,
they will sing his praises amidst flowers
while, somewhere, a cellar starts to flood,

and the housewife banging his front-door knocker
is not surprised to find him gone,
and runs for Thwaite, who's a better worker,
and sticks at a job until it's done.

BANK HOLIDAY

BRIGHT eyes in a pile of lumber
watching the spanking miles unroll
a seaside day in easy summer
    enter running or not at all
to the bodies without number
whoop of children swoop of gulls
    A lively tune on a tin whistle.

Blazing noon on a metal tangle
see the fat lady's skeleton mate,
Come and Get It, I'm No Angel,
    Kiss Me Quick Before It's Too Late;
Oh the bright and battering sandal
on the concrete's waste of heat
    Enter running or not at all.

Sandy mythologies by the mister
dribble nose and fly blown loose,
flags' and hands' heroic gestures;
    an old hat filling with booze
while the roaring roller coaster
flees its maze above the nudes
    Kiss me quick before it's too late.

Candy floss sticks, syrup waffles,
secret rides in the River Caves,
Scenes of the Harem, Sights Unlawful;
    widows and hucksters thick as thieves
and the day tilts at the bottle
and the starstruck girls believe.
    An old hat filling with booze.

Take me an air trip round the Tower
where, all glorious within,
spangles of the dancing floor
   shake a big bellyful of din
and balloons in splendid shower
fall to zips and hearts undone
   Widows and hucksters thick as thieves.

Rotherham Stockport Salford Nelson
Sheffield Burnley Bradford Shaw
roll by a shining Cinderella
   into the night's enormous maw,
smashin girl and luvly fella
tip the wink and close the door.
   Shake a big bellyful of din.

Sodden straws and french letters,
trodden ices, orange hulls,
clotted beach and crowded gutters.
   A lively tune on a tin whistle
sings to the sea 'What matters . . . matters'
and the street sweepers and the gulls,
   Into the night's enormous maw.

MRS. ROOT

BUSYBODY, nosey-parker
lacking the vast discretion of most
was this woman. The self-cast
chief mourner at funerals, worker
at weddings, she could sniff out death
in a doctor's optimism, joggle
a maiden's mind (button-holed on the front path)
till virginity bit like filed teeth.

Prepared, without discrimination,
friend and enemy for the grave.
Washed, talcumed them all. A woman
who wore such ceremonies like a glove,
could console a grief-struck household
that hardly knew her name, and then
collect money for a wreath fit to wield
at a Queen's passing. Death-skilled

but no less wedding-wise,
her hand stitched the perfecting dart
in bridal satin; she brought report
of cars arriving, clear skies
towards the church. They were her tears
(pew-stifled) from which the happiest
laughter billowed confetti outside the black doors.
Of best wishes, loudest were hers.

And nobody thanked her; Why doesn't
she mind her own business?, they said
who'd leant upon her. Crude and peasant-like
her interest in brides, and the dead.
I thought so too, yet still was loath
to add my voice, sensing that
my secret poems were like her actions: both
pried into love and savoured death.

POEM AT EASTER

THERE have been times a voice, loud,
beyond question, has spoken from a cloud.
Disbelievers have heard the walking dead
prophesy, utter praises; converted

by miraculous blindness, visions, proof
(sensibly such), have stripped off
jewels and reputations, gone from home
in draughty rags to certain martyrdom.

These trouble like erotic dreams
our days of politics, of surnames;
no voice speaks from the clouds of drifting dust,
the dead are crammed in mass graves, earth-fast,

can praise nothing. I who would
have wafer flesh, have wine blood,
see houseproud dogma folding away truth,
expedience preparing for a bloodbath.

Is there no single vision pure
enough to survive the silent uproar?

My nights are broken; I have seen the bedpost
gather the sparse moonlight, become the risen Christ.

AN EMPTY HOUSE

Doors bolted; windows dirt-bleared.
Was ever invitation sent
to cross this garden, vilely littered
with ashes, garbage, once-elegant

columned Olympians;—toppled, broken?
No; but rabid ignoramus,
feckless far-from-home, wise man
exceeding wisdom, and various

frustrated ghosts, hover, strut,
slouch, and scribble in these grounds.
Forgotten squatters, from mere habit
raising occasional, imploring, hands

in antic faith. A common blindness
fudges with wishes dead hope;
the towers are fallen that were topless;
nothing left but strife, wrought shape!

Some few, compelled by pride to seek
the truth, scream, curse, take poison,
weep until their hearts break,
peering on cobwebs, splendour gone.

The best, sad-eyed, quick with courage,
admit an ending. Gather, dustbin
their old love-letters, damp from the garage,
and leave to work, to father children.

THE BURGLARY

It's two o'clock now; somebody's pausing in the street
to turn up his collar. The night's black: distraught
with chimney-toppling wind and harsh rain—
see, the wet's soaking in on the end-gable,
and the frothing torrent, overspilling the broken drain,

accosts the pavement with incoherent babble.
There is the house we want: how easy to burgle,
with its dark trees, and the lawn set back from the road;
the owners will be in bed now—the old couple;
you've got the position of the safe?—Yes, I know the code.

The cock's going mad up there on the church steeple;
the wind's enormous—will it ever stifle;
still, its noise, and the rain's are with us, I daresay,
they'll cover what we make, if we go careful
round by the greenhouse, and in at the back way.

Here's the broken sash I mentioned;—no need to be fearful,
watch how I do it: these fingers are facile
with the practice I've had on worse nights than this.
I tell you, the whole thing's going to be a doddle:
the way I've got it worked out, we can't miss.

Although, God knows, most things turn out a muddle,
and it only confuses more to look for a moral.
Wherever I've been the wind and the rain's blown;—
I've done my best to hang on, as they tried to whittle
the name from the action, the flesh away from the bone,

but I think, sometimes, I'm fighting a losing battle.
So many bad nights; so many strange homes to burgle,
and every job done with a mate I don't know:—
oh, you're all right; I don't mean to be personal,
but when the day breaks, you'll have your orders, and go.

Then, the next time the foul weather howls in the ginnel;
when the slates slide, the brimming gutters gurgle;
there'll be another lad I've never seen before,
with the rest of the knowledge that makes the job possible
as I ease up a window or skeleton-key a door.

Still, it's my only life, and I've no quarrel
with the boss's methods;—apart from the odd quibble
about allowances and fair rates of pay,
or the difficult routes I often have to travel,
or the fact that I never get a holiday.

Most of the time, though, I'm glad of mere survival,
even at the stormiest hour of the darkest vigil.
. . . Here's the hall door; under the stairs, you said?
This one's easy, because the old folk are feeble,
and lie in their curtained room, sleeping like the dead.

Sometimes, believe me, it's a lot more trouble,
when you've got to be silent, and move as though through treacle.
Now hold your breath while I let these tumblers click . . .
I've done these many a time . . . a well known model;
one more turn now . . . Yes; that does the trick.

Nothing inside? The same recurrent muddle;
I think the most careful plan's a bloody marvel
if it plays you true, if nothing at all goes wrong.
Well, let's be off; we've another place to tackle
under the blown, black, rain; and the dawn won't be long

when the wind will drop, and the rain become a drizzle,
and you'll go your way. Leaving me the bedraggled
remnants of night, that walk within the head
long after the sun-shot gutters cease to trickle,
and I draw my curtains, and topple into bed.

THE RETURN

EMERGING from cloud in the mountain pass
amongst a few sheep that fled through the coarse grass,
he saw the tarn in the distance, like a dark glass

catching what little was left of light.
A map-check showed the route he had taken was right;
he should have been on the spur, but the error was slight

enough to be neither here nor there,
and the way down was scree; bland and bare,
though it shifted beneath him, scratching the smooth air.

the going was easy on the lower
slopes, but, suddenly aware that his mouth was sour,
tongue parched, body bruised and tired, his step became slower.

He thought, when I reach there, I'll get a bath,
and food and drink on a clean damask cloth;—
then he saw, winding away to the left, the path

they'd told him to look for. 'It leads', they had said,
'to a house where they'll make you welcome, and give you a bed,
but don't allow yourself to be interrogated.

'They may be curious; but we must warn
against any mention of the fight by the tithe barn,
or of the bloody betrayal by the side of the tarn.

'Of the message you carry, give no token,
nor of the other matters of which we have already spoken;
it would, perhaps, be wise to hide your gun in the bracken.

'And on no account linger more than a day,
though they show every kindness, plead with you to stay;
you'll still have a long way to go, and a difficult way

'before you drop at last to the coast,
and deliver the message to the commander of the outpost.
Unless you make reasonable haste, all may be lost.'

He reached the house as the first pale star
appeared, and saw through the open weathered door
bright firelight playing on the rough stone floor,

and on the flowers in a glass dome,
the hundred other familiar features of the room,
and on his mother saying: 'Are you glad to be home?'

Through wrenching pain, his mother's kiss,
his father's slow smile, he thought queerly: what is
the reason for my getting back as late as this?

Surely I've been gathering the sheep
up there on the hillside where it's rocky and very steep,
and the clints in the limestone are flower-filled and deep.

In bed that night, he dreamed of a barn,
a difficult, clouded, journey from cairn to cairn,
a desperate fight, and betrayal, by the side of a tarn,

but he rose early to milk the cow,
and about that time two of the sows were in farrow,
and the plough to mend, and the wheel off the wheelbarrow.

One afternoon, sharpening a scythe,
he remembered a message he'd been entrusted with;
and laughed at memory, twisting an old myth.

In winter he found a pistol in the grass,
rusted and ancient. As he took aim along the pass,
the tarn, in the broken sights, shone, like a dark glass.

ST. MARK'S, CHEETHAM HILL

DESIGNED to dominate the district—
God being nothing if not large
and stern, melancholic from man's fall
(like Victoria widowed early)—
the church, its yard, were raised on a plateau
six feet above the surrounding green.
There weren't many houses then; Manchester
was a good walk away. I've seen
faded photographs: the church standing
amidst strolling gentry, as though
ready to sail for the Empire's farthest parts;—
the union jack at the tower's masthead
enough to quell upstart foreigners and natives.
But those were the early days. The city
began to gollop profits, burst
outward on all sides. Soon,
miles of the cheapest brick swaddled landmarks,
the church one. Chimes that had used to wake
workers in Whitefield, died in near streets.

From our house—a part of the parish—
St. Mark's is a turn right, a turn left,
and straight down Coke Street past the 'Horseshoe'.
The raised graveyard—full these many years—
overlooks the junction of five streets;
pollarded plane trees round its edge,
the railings gone to help fight Hitler.
Adam Murray of New Galloway,
'Who much improved the spinning mule',
needs but a step from his tomb to peer in
at somebody's glittering television;
Harriet Pratt, 'A native of Derby',
might sate her judgement-hunger with chips
were she to rise and walk twenty yards.
The houses are that close. The church,
begrimed, an ugly irregular box

squatting above those who once filled it
with faith and praise, looks smaller now
than in those old pictures. Subdued
by a raincoat factory's bulk, the Kosher
Slaughter House next door, its dignity
is rare weddings, the Co-op hearse,
and hired cars full of elderly mourners.

The congregations are tiny these days;
few folk could tell you whether it's 'High' or 'Low';
the vicar's name, the times of services,
is specialized knowledge. And fear has gone;
the damp, psalmed, God of my childhood has gone.
Perhaps a boy delivering papers
in winter darkness before the birds wake,
keeps to Chapel Street's far side, for fear
some corpse interred at his ankle's depth
might shove a hand through the crumbling wall
and grab him in passing; but not for fear
of black religion—the blurred bulk
of God in drizzle and dirty mist,
or hooded with snow on his white throne
watching the sparrow fall.
                              Now, the graveyard,
its elegant wrought-ironwork wrenched,
carted away; its rhymed epitaphs,
urns of stone and ingenious scrolls,
chipped, tumbled, masked by weeds,
is used as a playground. Shouting children
Tiggy between the tombs.
                              On Saturdays
I walk there sometimes—through the drift
of jazz from open doors, the tide
of frying fish, and the groups of women
gossiping on their brushes—to see the church,
its God decamped, or dead, or daft
to all but the shrill hosannas of children

whose prayers are laughter, playing such parts
in rowdy games, you'd think it built
for no greater purpose, think its past
one long term of imprisonment.

There's little survives Authority's cant
that's not forgotten, written-off,
or misunderstood. The Methodist Chapel's
been bought by the Jews for a Synagogue;
Ukrainian Catholics have the Wesleyan's
sturdy structure built to outlast Rome—
which clings to its holy snowball down the street;
and men of the district say St. Mark's
is part of a clearance area. Soon
it will be down as low as rubble
from every house that squeezed it round,
to bed a motorway and a new estate.
Or worse: repainted, pointed, primmed—
as becomes a unit in town-planners'
clever dreams of a healthy community—
will prosper in dignity and difference,
the gardened centre of new horizons.

Rather than this, I'd see it smashed,
and picture the final splendours of decay:
Opposing gangs in wild 'Relievo',
rushing down aisles and dusty pews
at which the houses look straight in
past broken wall; and late-night drunkards
stumbling their usual short-cut home
across uneven eulogies, fumbling
difficult flies to pour discomfort out
in comfortable shadows, in a nave
they praise with founts, and moonlit blooms of steam.

THE HOUSE, AT NIGHT

THE first stranger stood at the green gate,
wearing my clothes, and leaning on a tree.
   The hour was late;
   the place mystery,
although the house had much the look of home.
His speech was broken, like an ancient wall:
'Long gone;—which way's come;—broken;—kept;—
   least of them all.'
   He faded as I stepped
across the threshold, where the mat said Welcome.

The second stranger knelt beside the fire;
turning he smiled, and smiling wore my face;—
   although attire
   so rich, such supple grace
(he moved to take my hand)—I've never owned.
His speech was both mellifluous and plain:
'Your room is ready sir; the bed is warm
   and, here again,
   you'll come to no more harm.'
His voice was musical, yet made no sound.

The third stranger occupied my bed;
his flesh—my body—held you close and still.
   His sleeping head,
   its splendid features ill-
defined, as though from long rest under earth,
lay mouthless there, but oh the shadows spoke
his dreaming phrases, passionate and proud.
   'The spell is broken:
   night! night! night enshroud
all restless sleepers in the season's wrath.'

24

I turned away. The mirror held no light,
but, bright, within the final stranger stood;
   strange to my sight
   yet brother to my blood
since round his wounded form, perplexities
of day and night and twilight licked like flame,
and when he spoke I knew that voice my own.
   'I am your name:
   in suffering, alone.
Enter my kingdom; exorcize your furies.'

DECORATING IN APRIL

THE time before I came was trapped
   to inhabit the wafer-world between
   layers of paint. Now my knife has undone
   it, bared it to the spring air, and sun.
The window-frame's final coat is stripped,

but I'm no good workman whose mind
   cleaves to the close task. I rock
   violently on the ladder, shake—
   like a blind dog—a head gone dark,
and am unborn again, unmanned

for a split second, before that spirit
   of all I had no part in, ups
   to my eye's corner, billows and slips
   over the hedge, in the changing shapes
of cigarette smoke, and nonsense I inherit.

A SONG AT THE END

CHOPSLOPPING, winking, leering, nodding
   yes yes yes and fiddledeedee,
Death, you promiscuous busybody,
   try as you will you'll not catch me.

The scruffy-plumed raven may ogle me under,
   bing bong bang your greetings explode,
leanly catastrophe lick at my shoulder,
   suavely your mannequins model my shroud;

I don't give a damn that you've buried me decent
   R.I.P. in the local gazette;
such subtle persuasion is hardly a reason
   to give up the ghost, and I'm not dead yet.

Nor ever will be while the wind is my whistle,
   the moon a young woman, the ocean a tear;
I'm off like a shot from a well-oiled pistol
   with nothing but terror to set against fear.

Garrulous street will you muffle my hurry?
   which way what way how way now;
say that I hitched a lift in a lorry,
   say that I sailed in a leak-riddled scow.

Say that the heavens grew lips, and enticed me
   up up up till only my shoes
stuck from a cloud like a sign unsightly,
   say that I've gone to haggle with Jews.

Say the Magician of Insects changed me
   back to a beetle he crushed underfoot;
say I saw visions, that they deranged me
   and sent me to bed with a foul-mouthed slut.

Say I went running in every direction:
    up down sideways and to and fro,
say that I babbled of dissatisfaction,
    and wanted the management to know.

And tell HIM I said I was going for ever.
    The ends of the earth and the depths of the sea,
the universe, even, is a cock's stride over,
    but try as he will he'll not catch me.

PORTO VENERE

Amidst many bronzed women's thighs,
slack, long, on hot rock,
the Poet is remembered. His motto
does not disturb, in three languages:
'Great . . . Brave . . . Who swam the gulf . . .
In memory of his inspiration, this grotto'.

Below, the sea clubs rock, bursts,
streams back through stains and lichens
to fierce sky-paling blue; above,
fig trees loll from the castle wall—
a monument to outworn causes,
where the inheriting ant and tourist move.

History's marginalia. Here
called galleys from Gaul; Byzantines added
a few arches, forgotten graves;
Genoese built grandly over all,
and Byron wrote a minor poem
before, or after daring these sulky waves—

though that's apocryphal. In the Gulf,
ruffled to Lerici, the sea
shimmers in mile-long creases. Flame
on the farther shore consumed Shelley,
the youth indubitably drowned;—
there is a restaurant which bears his name.

APOLOGUE

HAVING a fine new suit,
and no invitations,
I slept in my new suit
hoping to induce
a dream of fair women.

And did indeed: the whole night long,
implored by naked
beauty—pink on white linen—
I struggled to remove
my fine new suit.

At dawn I awoke, blear-eyed;
sweating beneath encumbering rags.

AT A HOTEL

PERHAPS that was the most
appropriate place of all,
for only late-coming drunkards
prowled in the deserted passages,
where the living cared least, and the dead
could not be expected to call,
pouring in the midnight ear
their usual muddling messages.
What they had gone there for
that night neither of them knew,
though both devised ritual
music to name the occasion.
When he came to her room she thought
it important that the carpet was blue,
while he saw clearly their naked
nearness, and summoned up passion.
Knowing little of love,
much less of innocence,
they lay in a dark heat
without ecstasy or shame,
both bowing and scraping
in a palace of self-pretence,
whose king had no face, and whose
courtiers were blind and lame—
she at a ceremony,
he too in a crowded hall
where drunken revellers exchanged
intimate, incoherent, messages:

outside the uninvited,
who could not be expected to call,
waited, dumbly waited,
in the ill-lit deserted passages.

'The moon, my love, deceives, O many, many,'
    He says. She says:
    'Then let us not look up;'
kissing his shadowed face, turning her money.

'I was long since lost in the deserts of women,'
    He says. She says:
    'Lie down in this cool place,'
and strokes his lips, her hand as slow as famine.

'Has the wind dropped? Is that the rain falling?'
    He says. She says:
    'Tighten your arms around me;
it is only the stars' flight, the earth rolling.'

'And will this night, then, not go on for ever?'
    He says. She says:
    'Quiet my love, be quiet;
sleep is full of bad dreams but will soon be over.'

A BOOK OF BEASTS

He favours dumbness in most subjects,
that none bears witness against his words,
harrying precious articulation
with passion's other speech. The bull,
the dog, the parakeet, the lizard,
lie neatly at hand to make his points.

Museum and memory, strolled for purpose
of wit's exercise, have them lit—
the possible poems, stuffed to the life;
many move at the touch of a switch;
grunt, bark, tweet, hiss, after their kind—
but all in ordered sequence, muted

beneath the only human voice—
which won't be interrupted. Sure
of his own refinement swagger and flair,
urbane, for that, from the Sixth Day,
he is undoubtedly Lord of Creation,
with such a bestiary in his briefcase.

THE LOOK OF LOVE

BELEAGUERED by passions, as by thunder
of encircling arms, some ate dirt,
became louse-ridden, waxed holy
by degrees of deprivation
and fits of weakness; withstood the hordes,
entertained not their grinning Gods,
and died virgins, at length, slowly.

Some explored a metaphor
nearer to home. Local affections,
pursued through fog, a maze of streets,
finally left them, dazed and tricked,
writing, in lieu of love poems,
a pocket guide to their own district.

Saints and fools. Some, who were neither,
(like you and I) bit lips in kisses,
groaned beneath weight of thrusting flesh,
or tried to deal gently with another.
To these the scale of things was plain;
but *they* surrendered, gathered fat
like foreign honours, or went out
to the corner shop and were never seen again.

THE CONQUERORS

WITH brisk walks, bromide, cold baths,
we have rid ourselves of persistent myths;
night's verminous infestations
of dream shrivel, die—and most passions.

Unless to obey be such: the ache
for orders and supervised hard work:
(to long grass bending small scissors,
from crumpled leather, rubbed mirrors.)

Hands at the stainless gates of sense
withdraw, placated by crusts, odd pence,
for these things we would give. The sentry
breathes into gloves; the night is wintry,

the people cowed and curfewed. We
govern a sullen land. The enemy
clenches in darkness, pride, fevers,
visions of judgement, dead lovers,

and memory's brute cries. Untold
his lice. Already we have unveiled
the foyer of the future, heated
by solar cells, austerely appointed—

there is no looking back. At first light,
as newly mounted, the guard turns out;
Unmarked by night those rigid faces
blank-eyed before the blancoed hoses.

THE CROFT

THE croft, shadowed between houses,
blotchy with grass like fading bruises,
had hardly ground to be called croft,
being no more than an unclaimed cleft

in a grubby, once stately, row
of four-window fronts done in stucco.
Shut like a world in a glass ball
this is where childhood befell

whatever it is that's stepped on
into my moving imagination.
Name, purpose, family face,
were vivid daydreams of that place,

where, ear cocked to the sour earth
and the scavenging rats' scratch beneath
in caved cellars, my mind embodied
populous otherwheres to be studied;

a God who, if he cared to come,
might broken-glass-top wall that kingdom,
or (since an old Jew, who retailed fish
there before his shop was demolished)

might sell the burst mattress, the frames
of bike and umbrella, and the bones
buried by dogs, even the mind
that summoned him from the back of the wind.

The real abides; the poem finds it.
By instinct: cat or dog-wit
of sniff and sixth sense, the poem
follows its own secret way home.

Time, that had shored, crumbles. The years,
their accreted populous otherwheres,
vanish, and I alone am left,
I and the poem and the croft

too close for distinction. Rats beneath
scurry and squeak; from his burst mouth
the ever-present God speaks—
innocuous rhetoric of wet kapok.

WITH LOVE SOMEHOW

To tell, my nearest possible dear,
myself to you, close caught in my telling;
in words humble as your collected self
put down in nakedness for me upon this sheet—
I have not trust enough to dare, who hides
behind—always, the blizzard's blank splendour;
bearing—always, the extravagant, bountiful,
teeming curse of summer. No way of word
where metaphors don't matter.

Yet, since the day lies careless on the floor,
let me attempt far more than I can bare,
or ever say when dressed to kill.
My giants all were foundlings once;
I've come on mysteries, and taken in
unreasoning things that grew to chuck me out.
So every father sees a candle-sun,
enormous seas peopled with strangers,
or dies lost in his own superfluousness.

The poem waves goodbye, bolts the door,
and settles down by the exiled poet's fireside.

These, to this conjunction apposite,
are few of many that I cannot name.
I'd have the restless rest unrave itself
but in that element I am not here.

On one night, love, from every word flung
in the grinding teeth that tear away
the loving from our lust, we loosed
an anarchy of rioting seasons.
Not that the mistaken, the broken, were more
than wanderers in unconsecrated latitudes;
no saints or cosmic jokers—certainly not
in my uncertain calendar had they any day,
or name, or claim upon anybody's poem.

As such so's are, I sent me out:
shorebound, we all watch fading landlights
stamp our banishment.
I dreamed a death among the violent islands,
and yet the waters, death-grey indeed,
bore me, torn and ten-year taunted,
towards green sleep and true Penelope.
. . . Or that's some saying (garbled myth or mine)
I find a fisted truth in. Not in this
bed though, not this bed. No;
this time I came this time's way, as—
my dear, will you believe it?—we all must,
and none the worse or better for it.

And the flesh! Bird-beast compelled
to ruin in its sight, caught in a grandiose flight,
teach—contrive me to your grace;
or, magic, drown entirely in the slopped pot,
the fumbling sweat sucked fingers
stinking towards their bloody genesis.

The bed we lay on, like a graven stone
turned on the water. Yet not at all:
the ear confirms the land, and hears the whirr
from miles of bus-routes winding a cocoon
around an unimportant fornication.
On draughty seats ride memories of home,
. . . which we may not forget.
The cold baker, paying in kind; prostitute;
and printer with tomorrow's news,
proud of his difference: all share our night,
must be remembered in the bed's fierce images.

And yet my head cranes backward to provide
a known perspective for the wrath I ride.

Again, where I began, with you my kind child;
and how to say more than a straight thrust
and little delicacies; as true and traitorous

as from that lost first. Heroic couplings
to those without shadows; ours shake
broken bedsprings in their myopic dance
and I'm as fickle as this tongue.

But hear across the wandered waste between
our impossible dreams, my dear,
oh hear in that exhausting wilderness
where stands only a tree spilling
no useful seed on anything beneath,
and the bee—lunatic in an unseasoned land—
shrivels to powder in its honeycomb,
my slipshod coming, Long boned and undermanned
across a litter of like, cared for at least,
on kind seas in my own season.

I taste your tongue in the silence.
Once more the words I sent to dredge
about my dark return, to taunt my ears
in riddling sequence from the room of love
whose randy lightnings flare me to the end.
Nothing this night will (or can, I think)
say or unsay itself. I am only myself
and all others since ever,
despaired of in what is none of me,
and grieving; oh, my distant darling, grieving.

MAN TO MAN

. . . for all this, they outlast us.
Think of the merry widows, grandmas,
and local aged crones
who've buried—how many was it?

Outwit us on the way.
Early with: 'Nice boys don't do that',
later with drooping eyelids, close mouths,
lastly with children, backache, times of the month.

Which of us has not suffered—
Medusa'd to stony silence,
or leg-locked right outside
Aphrodite's blissful smile?

No wonder saints do without them!
You can't believe hell (or heaven)
is elsewhere with *them* at your elbow—
or tell, precisely, which is which.

DEATH AT NIGHT

TOWARDS your purpose (if may be judged
a purpose here, where signatures fade
quickly, instructions are soon smudged
beyond comprehension) give your word.

For her sake, too. This much is certain:
pretend as much for her sake,
whose hand has beckoned you, drawn the curtain,
who waits now, naked in the dark.

Your need will sanctify her bed.
Or tell this to yourself. Be wholly
engrossed by lips; concerned to feed
her, or else the appetite of folly.

Then darkness take her face. Wet flesh
shudder beneath you and confuse
mind with body, caress with whiplash,
protean power with straight issues.

You know how she will lie, will look,
when bronchial morning counts the dead
and bustles the live home: awake
as you are never; gathered, uncovered

as you cannot be. She will rise
(tell this yourself) secure in love,
and heavy-footed with firm purpose
will fill the kettle, light the stove.

COMMUNITY SINGING

GRANDAD Connor toiled at the forge
   may his bones dance his bones sing,
his heart was shrunk but his lust large,
he tricked at cards and worshipped God
kept his wife in perennial pod
butter he ate and the rest marge,
   A straight street and nothing in sight.

Uncle Henry trained as a clerk
   may his bones dance his bones sing,
to sit on his arse was too much like work;
one morning he stayed steady in bed
and lay supine till the day he died;
some men won't leave a thing to luck
   A straight street and nothing in sight.

This was our Jack, and Auntie Prue
   may their bones dance their bones sing,
both had serious tasks to do
Jack went daft with a hell of a fuss
and Prue fell under a fifty-five bus
the family grave excused the two
   A straight street and nothing in sight.

Cousin Arthur followed the dogs
   may his bones dance his bones sing,
natty his bow and Oxford Bags
cute the monogram on his shirts
oh what a hit with the classy skirts;
struck down on a night of jig-a-jigs
   A straight street and nothing in sight.

Dad was a lad with a golden tongue
   may his bones dance his bones sing,
went overboard at the siren's song

left his heart on a butcher's slab
swopped his beads for a pack of tabs
said he wouldn't be gone long
   A straight street and nothing in sight.

Here's a prayer for all the lot,
   may their bones dance their bones sing.
The blossom must fall to form the fruit,
Troy was sacked for a third-rate verse
a woman's pout and a toy horse;
torn-up Orpheus twang that lute,
   A straight street and nothing in sight.

NOVEMBER NIGHT

THE fire roars in the boiler-back,
   pots and pans in neat rows
   swell in the lamplight's friendly shadows,
tomorrow's shirt hangs from the rack.

Trails at my ear a turned-back cuff,
   as though in assurance, this shirt:
   yesterday's stains, yesterday's dirt,
unknown to such starched, immaculate stuff.

A gilded hand grasps paid-up bills
   prettily, on a gleaming hook,
   in the cupboard a fragrant cake
waits to be cut, the kettle boils.

The house murmurs; its peace abounds
   with suave civilities. I have heard
   much quiet insistence: 'All is mastered:
beds have been warmed, the clocks wound,

dead men tucked tight in earth,
   their errors with them; rest your head,
   for, see—all is cared-for, tidied.'
Nodding a Yes not come to mouth,

yet must I prowl from room to room,
   upstairs and down, in dark corners
   where damp exudes, cellar-brick furs,
and old dust piles in the rafter's gloom;

and must I heave these curtains wide
   upon fog, like a blind wall
   hemming the house. Neither voice nor footfall
sounds from the nothingness outside,

nor is there warmth of blanket's load
  can pinion my sleep tonight from cold
  nightmares of flight through windows sealed
against the encasing death of God.

OCTOBER IN CLOWES PARK

THE day dispossessed of light. At four oclock
in the afternoon, a sulphurous, manufactured
twilight, smudging the scummed lake's far side,
leant on the park. Sounds, muffled—
as if the lolling muck clogged them at the source—
crawled to the ear. A skyed ball thudded
to ground, a swan leathered its wings by the island.
I stood and watched a water-hen arrow
shutting silver across the sooty mat
of the lake's surface, an earl's lake,
though these fifty years the corporation's,
and what is left of the extensive estate—
a few acres of scruffy, flat land
framing this wet sore in the minds of property agents—
a public park. All else is built on.
Through swags of trees poked the bare backsides
of encircling villas, garages, gardening-sheds,
a ring of lights making the park dimmer.
Boys and men shouldering long rods—
all licensed fishers, by their open way—
scuffled the cinders past me, heading for home,
but I stayed on; the dispossessed day
held me, turned me towards the ruined Hall.
Pulsing in that yellow, luminous, murk
(a trick of the eye), the bits of broken pillar
built into banks, the last upright wall,
the stalactite-hung split shells of stables,
seemed likely to find a voice—such pent-in grief
and anger!—or perhaps to explode silently
with force greater than any known to progress,
wiping the district, town, kingdom, age,
to darkness far deeper than that which fluffed
now at the neat new urinal's outline,
and heaved and beat behind it in the ruins.
Like a thud in the head, suddenly become memory,
stillness was dumb around me. Scrambling up

47

a heap of refuse, I grabbed at crystalled brick.
Flakes fell from my hand—a gruff tinkle—
no knowledge there of what brought the Hall low,
or concern either. Neither did I care.
Irrecoverably dead, slumped in rank weed
and billowy grass, it mouldered from here to now,
connoting nothing but where my anger stood
and grief enough to pull the sagging smoke
down from the sky, a silent, lethal, swaddling
over the garden I played in as a child,
and over those children—laughter in the branches—
shaking the pear-tree's last sour fruit to ground.

A BALLAD OF LOST AND FOUND

THE words I'd have you know me by
  are sullen and slow to hand;
for many I forced to the last bonfire,
  and some in rain and wind

walk dirty streets I left for dead,
  or take the cadger's bite
with folk whose homes I thought ill-known,
  lit by the sour gas-light.

There's some the old dog scrabbled deep
  down on the brickyard croft,
and some in the lunatic asylum,
  delicate and daft.

But listen to those I muster now!
  Though Uncle Harry's gone
to slit the guts of Almighty God,
  his fool's cap I put on.

His bells I shake, his bladder bang,
  as night falls in a heap.
Let's look at the way our manhood hangs
  before we come to sleep.

Was it a thousand years ago
  I gave my head three twists,
paired off the feet to fit these legs,
  the hands to suit these wrists,

tapped at my heart to make it tick.
  pulled from my arse the cork,
and sprang from the tide that foams beside
  this awful other dark?

Or was it yesterday, at tea,
   creation shoved me forth?
I saw my mother look at me
   like my own birth.

(Some, on an outing from the Works
   fell when the crowd roared,
and some in a brothel near All Saints'
   were pinched by an old bawd).

Leastwise, the place I'm at is known
   to all that have an ear
for the sound of the lodger in the attic,
   the beetle in the floor;

and those with eyes may see me plain,
   flustered to faith by tits,
bound by a woman's shaking legs,
   and scarred with love-bites.

You can touch me up if your finger's fine:
   this is a feeling day.
(Some were arrested in the square
   for gross indecency.)

Or follow your nose. I say the smell
   of pain's to this place.
I cut off my head with a carving knife,
   and still my ears ache.

You'll know the house, whose falling walls
   catastrophe can't budge;
and maybe the mog with the mangled ear
   sat on the window-ledge.

Perhaps I'll be writing an Ode to Love,
   or emptying the slops,
disputing the price of jelly-babies
   at Bracegirdle's shop,

perhaps I'll be blacking the mirror's eye,
    or calling mam a bitch.
(And some for fifty years' service
    were given a gold watch.)

Whatever I'm on you'll find me here
    a simple lad at heart,
with a smile for you; for authority
    an ever-ready fart.

I fill in a perm on Friday night,
    fidget about at Mass,
and wander round the graveyard
    to find which tomb it was

I burst from, once—I think it was Easter,
    I know the guards were boozed.
(Some, by turning common informer,
    kept their palms greased.)

Logos Sophia, was I then,
    at crack of cock about?
there's room for every theory here,
    for every theory's doubt.

There's room for the man with the black book
    and the witch-burning eyes;
I fellowed him in the naafi queue
    when I was Lord of Flies.

Aye, Jack, I fell with a hell of a wound
    the night before the peace.
They decked me up in bunting and
    a flag across my face.

Not that I fret: the like of me's
    meat for the like of you;—
and you are meat for the like of me,
    I see it on your brow.

So down at the 'Horseshoe' get them in,
    for I'll be there direct.
On cribbage board and dart board
    we'll play the final act.

Then with my love I'll lie the last
    before the judgement shout;
she's such a charm will keep me warm
    and suck the poison out

though Armageddon stalks the night,
    bloody and black as death.
(Some on the breathless road to love
    drowned in a rubber sheath;

and some when Uncle Harry went,
    jumped in the yellow van.
Some in a maze of ways and means
    forgot why they began).

But here's the supper table laid:
    we'll keep the frost out yet;
hang your clothes on the cellar door
    and gob all you can eat.

This meal I meant for starving hordes,
    leprous, blind, and lame,
half expecting the world, tonight—
    but only you came,

and the blood of my father at the door:
    O pity, let it in!
That's you, and me, and my father's blood,
    and the madness I put on

to take the blessing and hear the toast
    from my five dumb throats.
Some in search of a better job
    were speared with banknotes.

and some the old dog scrabbled deep
down on the brickyard croft;
and some, preposterous and gay,
looked in my heart and laughed.

THE clown's chaos surrounds him; miracles
    balance on single wheels,
or, skeletal, puff in astonished blubberings
    outward in all directions.
He ascends into Heaven balloon-like,
    fashions a joke of heart-break.

Called mountebank to his obvious
    false nose, teardrops course
globules of glycerine down his face;
    when you turn in disgust
he pinches your bottom, sticks his tongue out,
    pushes from shore in a small boat

to quell a tempest, or step on to water.
    A notice saying: 'Pure'
is plastered across his worst obscenities;
    his heart is endorsed officially
with false trademarks, and plastic seals
    guaranteeing him King of Fools.

Nevertheless, when all are in bye-byes
    his nerves follow the highways
towards Orion, towards Andromeda;
    nor do his fingers falter
stretching the paper to satisfaction
    upon hoops of resurrection.

At dawn to earth again. Disciples,
    appearing like mushroom-stools,
perish ungathered, while he for evening's
    orgy of simple fun
flexes the rubber penis, paints on hands
    and feet careful nail-wounds.

A JOURNAL OF BAD TIMES

In Autumn, begin.
                    Uprooting geraniums,
shaking them gently for storage in darkness,
had heard guns crackle in far streets.
In the deepening sky, one evening,
an airman wrote 'Love'—a vaporous trail
gone before sunset.
                    Beyond the city, mountains;
most often hidden. On clear days certain fields,
a pike, glinting glass. Many went that way,
wheels rumbling towards rock.
                              None saw a good end.
The last birds flew late. South, eagerly
when they went; still, sparrows at my door
importuned for what bread?

    Guard against draughts; bolt the banging door.

Sat late by small oil, a moth, and one moment's silence.
Books helped me, so did other things:
crossword puzzles; meditation.
                    November rain
stained the chimney breast;
at night the wounded groaned beyond the hedge.
The sink froze.
                All day long the tanks clattered past,
disturbing earth, churning up cobbles;
not a face I knew; guns pointing onward.

    Christmas is nothing without a child.

Ghosts again in the front room.
I thought they'd gone for good, but meaning no harm.
Seeking their own echoes, I think;
their faces in mirrors.

And then. . . .
New men with the first green shoots;
declarations; manifestoes; promises
in shoddy eccentric type on grey paper.
'There will be public trials . . .

                    full restitution . . .'
Dreamed often: four friends dead;
one in exile; one a traitor to some cause;
but could not say the rest.
After the big winds the battle came back;

                    muddled,
beyond the understanding of many.
The snipers stayed longest,

              and the sky brightened,
imperceptively, towards summer.
Twigs from laburnum cluttered the front path;
one branch snapped abruptly while I watched,
suggesting more death.

   Sharpen the good saw.

Noticed willowherb in unlikely places:
on the roofs of lavatories; in formal gardens.
Dock leaf and dandelion brightened the ruins
beyond my care.

             The cat went out; never came back,
but the strawberries ripened well; this gave pleasure.
In the topmost room, the lodger, enfeebled,
scrabbled the quilt, called for a priest,

                or rabbi.
Only a lay preacher came, and he starved and rambling.

   Trim the hedge; sweep the cellar; send letters.

One day it was over, or seemed to be;

             someone said
a van with a loudspeaker telling good news . . .
I think someone said that; and near the end

the birds came back; or perhaps they just came out
to see August with the din of brass-bands,
flaunting banners, throwing down arms in the street.
How the children shouted!
                              How the women cried!
I smiled in the garden, clutching a dead root,
and the thrush stood on the aerial opposite,
singing! singing!
                    Old friends returned;
drank my new wine;
                         I welcomed them home.

FOR A LOST GIRL

I

To fake compassion, fix,
  arrange, and supervise
a cosmos free from shocks,
  scaled to a stage's size,

she bathed her body clean,
  deodorized and douched,
that she should be, again,
  man-handled but untouched.

Easier this, by far,
  than the hot bull's breath,
those horns intent to gore
  her singleness to death;

or than a world in which
  compassion must be learned
from Love, the cross-patch
  as often halt as horned.

Now she has scripts to read,
  committees to attend,
ideas to fill her head,
  polite, admiring, friends,

and all the world's a stage.
  The King is Dead. Long Live
The Queen, to whom our age
  shall ample homage give.

II

Since body's lost its knack—
    which was the death of your opinions,
    and all have come back
resurrected, annotated, strung into sermons
    without loophole or crack—

I own no weapon strong
    enough to hold in sure subjection
    the devil of your tongue,
bred from your doltish reason's predilection
    for what is neat, and wrong.

Goodbye, goodbye my dear;
    more thoughtful men than I may suffer
    your intellect's career,
may grow obese on that asexual wafer
    proffered without a tear.

For me you sobbed beneath
    crucified man while dumbing darkness
    plundered the freight of breath,
fused the brain's circuits to violent blackness.
    That, was a good death.

IV

If you would have it sole criterion—
    the upthrust in your belly—let me go;
eyes roll white for some other, stay
    at finishing school for ever when I'm gone.

But know, this biter of your breasts, lord
    of your loins, grew from such a loud stock,
that was no sensuous essay, no sex-trick,
    but what generations in his ears roared

of love and death. You will not find its match
  in any bed where love's a lesser pain,
or where you're worshipped, or where simpler men
  importune you with love that's pure, not hotch-potch.

Seek (if ever sickened by girlhood's ease
  of animal joy, and answers that come pat)
a man who, like me, trails his fool's coat
  only to hood his thought; whose eyes, from yours,

turn blankly, at odd times, towards rooms
  you cannot visit. His thrust with fire and flood
enough to raze your proud state will be powered,
  and if he leaves your arms to write poems,

or raise his family dead, be glad that he
  is troubled so, for to your bed he'll bring
creation's endless comedy in the strong
  heave of his arse, his longing to be free.

V

  Those are no doves about her head:
    wings blacken the sun, sharp beaks
  raven on flesh at noonday,
    cannot be sated. She stalks

  cloud-high her travelling nightmare
    in every lover's bed, laughs
  soundless sheet-lightning, doffs
  innocence to act the whore

  and, sweetly tousled at dawn, sleeps
    by your naked side. From her eyes,
  minute and unheroic, stares
    your own self at you, as she cries

60

and seeks your lips, shaking with fear
at such a dream of the male sea
and of her drowning. Glad that you
are strong, and comfortingly near.

VI

Is this the room you live in? This
freezing space where sentences fall
straight from the mouth to deep graves?
I thought you had a home.

A girl who wore such flesh as yours,
but differently, used to live here.
the furniture, the pictures are the same,
but now look blind and deaf.

What can I do but go away,
knowing no word of Love or Spring
that death would cherish. No token
of my common foolishness.

VII

PORTO VENERE

One midnight, glittering-eyed, in restless silence,
she left our bed, the tower where we were lodged,
and hurried to the sea. The moon was full.
Over the lanterns in the square, the dancing
couples who'd stay till dawn, it swung seaward
through legions of tiny clouds; and she—high-breasted
beside the harbour's fidget of clunking boats—
blanched and burrowed among the shifting shadows,
hearing only the lonely grotto's roar—
like the moon's voice, or the voice of her own blood.

I did not see her go, but dozed heavy
with wine under the wounds of a pallid icon,
and dreamed her body clung so close to mine
spindrift of sweat scattered from huge surges
of muscled battering, undertow sucked back
surfacing faces, thrust, and filled, and killed
everything but the sea's; until she lay
salty and heavy-eyed within my arms,
murmuring: 'Love, the waves, the waves were awful.
The moon went in. I thought that I might drown.'

VIII

Well-met, we two warring crowns,
    to join distinguished battle;
let there be cries of triumph, groans—
    no boring tittle-tattle

of pretence that this King, this Queen,
    might come to terms, might settle
sanely the blood bad with spleen,
    or lick each other's spittle.

For you and I have long known,
    —black of the pot and kettle—
we fight for right of life and throne
    against an equal mettle.

So throw back the bedding, lie down,
    and let us to the battle;
we'll prove who wears the greater crown—
    if both must die like cattle!

X

You—whose own flesh is your despair,
whose heart's grown-up enough to hate
its vagaries, but not to control them,
whose love—escaped its one strong leash—
rampages here, there, everywhere,

crying itself to sleep in beds
you have no knowledge of, or hope—
be quiet for me; learn stillness.
Not claiming more than any man
(being the brute force, and Gods

foolish and fond, which make you such
a torment to yourself), is wise
to claim; but poet, clown, and lover—
for his troubles far from your bed—
I pen these wooden words as crutch

under your weakness, thumb my nose,
tumble and joke, to point the wit
of self-known human silly kind,
and will not shed a single tear
for fear you'll strike the tragic pose

of raving to ruin. Dear, all lips
are much the same in darkness, mine
no different, perhaps, for being mine,
but I have eyes to recommend me,
keen to your smallest mole, and hopes

you'll mystify always, since I am
he who is gifted with you whole.
Be still. No novelties suffice
where custom, truth, and puzzlement
cleave together to make a home.

63

XI

My Love who last night, the destroyer
   of ordered settlements, swung her breasts
to crash down trees, and sturdily housed
   communities trod to the ground beneath her flat-footed power,

this morning, Queen among her people,
   weeps for the homeless, visits death
and succours the dying—grim with grief
   that God has seen fit to visit her reign with such trouble.

XII

I love you as I love the world,
   turning away often to retch
bile and bits I cannot hold

in guts grown gross on the rich
   diet of thirty years. Goddess—
naked or clothed—wife, bitch,

woman forever anonymous,
   known only by your open thighs
moist beneath mine in pitch darkness,

will you be content with lies—
   darling, my dear darling sweetheart—
that I should love you less than this

grave-ridden place in which I'm set—
   down, amidst stinking histories,
with all the wombs of earth to brat?